KRAMER THE KING

EVELYN WASSERMANN

AuthorHouse™
1663 Liberty Drive
Bloomington, IN 47403
www.authorhouse.com
Phone: 833-262-8899

This book is printed on acid-free paper.

ISBN: 978-1-6655-6497-7 (sc)
ISBN: 978-1-6655-6499-1 (hc)
ISBN: 978-1-6655-6498-4 (e)

Library of Congress Control Number: 2022913110

Print information available on the last page.

Published by AuthorHouse   02/02/2024

authorHOUSE®

Illustrations by the fabulous team at Authorhouse.

Thanks to my friends and mentors, Judith and
Brian, for their expertise and patience.

INTRODUCTION

The house on Station Lane holds three
Two old cats and kind Miss E
Tucker and Onyx are sister and brother
Who never wanted to have another
Yet six years later Kramer came
And the house would never be the same!
Kramer, Kramer, blond and strong
Found everything at the house all wrong
Putting his nose in everything
Acting as if he were the King
Selfish and spiteful, as you will see
The story unfolds and you will surely AGREE!

MONDAY

High on the counter top was Kramer's plate
When food was served, he was never late
Tucker and Onyx sat way below
Their empty bowls all in a row
For Kramer had already gobbled their food
Putting those two in a very foul mood
They whimpered, they simpered
They moaned, and they groaned
And prayed that King Kramer…
Would be DE-THRONED!

TUESDAY

Just like every other pet
Kramer had to see the vet
Kramer got so very wild
Acting like a vicious child
Bit the doctor on her coat
When she tried to check his throat
Jumped upon the office scale
Broke the scope and tore the mail
Kramer, Kramer took the stand
Showing who was in command
And --- wiped the doctor OUT!

WEDNESDAY

One bright sunny springtime day
Miss E took Kramer out to play
She zipped the cat inside her jacket
But Kramer began to make a racket
Scaring the birds in a nearby tree
Startling a neighbor who was drinking tea
He suddenly lunged out from her arm
Putting Miss E into great alarm
Kramer, Kramer, nowhere to be found
Not in the tree tops, not on the ground
Not behind bushes, not in the stream
Causing Miss E to let out a scream
At nightfall Miss E returned home alone
Only to find Kramer BACK ON HIS THRONE!

6

THURSDAY

Guests were invited for cookies and tea
And sat in the parlor with kind Miss E
Kramer decided he needed attention
Since no one was giving him an Honorable Mention
He went inside their purses, around their feet
Under their skirts, on top of their seats
But the ladies continued to chat with Miss E
Ignoring King Kramer's ongoing plea
Then suddenly Kramer sat down with a smile
For on the clean rug was a steaming hot pile
Attention he wanted; attention he got
Causing Miss E to yell quite A LOT!

8

FRIDAY

"Everything in the house is mine, mine, mine
That's how I like it; it's really just fine
The table, the bag, the ledge, and the chairs
The lamp, and the sink, and the mat near the stairs"
By this time Onyx had had enough
Of Kramer always invading his stuff
He'd sit on the couch, and the King would cry "Mine!"
He'd curl up near the bed, and again he'd hear "Mine!"
"Mine! Mine! Mine!" each and every single time
So Onyx decided it was time for a fight
And beat up old Kramer with all of his might
He sat right down in Kramer's spot
And growled and swung his paws a lot
Then Kramer came to claim his throne
He scratched poor Onyx and made him groan
And pounced right on him with a big loud 'Plop!'
And cried out wildly "I'M STILL ON TOP!"

SATURDAY

At feeding time on Station Lane
Kramer, Tucker, Onyx each get the same
All three bowls get filled to the top
Yet Kramer eats from each non-stop
"Stop it, Kramer!" shouts Miss E
"You won't get away from me!"
Yet lickety-split he's not to be found
And he disappears without even a sound
He finds a cozy hideaway
Making the laundry his place to stay
Then he discovers the high TV
"I'll never be found by old Miss E!"
Later he hops on the toilet seat
Tail in the tank and ready to greet---
EVERYONE!
Spraying water in every face
Making a mess of the entire place
Up on his hind legs, proud and tall
But the Lion King is about to FALL!

SUNDAY

Kramer, Kramer, thought he could fly
Climbed up the staircase, so very high
Suddenly fell to the downstairs floor
Kramer, Kramer, KING NO MORE!
Onyx and Tucker fly to the scene
Gleefully trying not to be mean
Seeing King Kramer bumped off his throne
Crown off his head – now all alone
Sent to the vet for his bruises and breaks
Everything hurts him, everything aches
Bandaged and collared and wanting to hide
Yet wishing the others would come to his side
He's humbled and ready to make amends
With Tucker and Onyx, his newfound *friends*
Gone Kramer's kingdom, his crown and his key
But now in its stead there's a CAT FAMILY!

EPILOGUE

The house on Station Lane holds three
Two old cats and kind Miss E
Tucker and Onyx are sister and brother
Who now have Kramer AND one another!

AUTUMN

Now the house on Station Lane holds four
Three old cats, old Miss E. … NO ROOM FOR MORE!
It's been six months since Kramer's fall
And the King no longer stands so tall.
Tucker and Onyx have found their places
And there's no more fighting – no more races.
Warming the heart of old Miss E.
The cats have become a FAMILY.
They sit atop the windowsill
Unusually quiet, unusually still
Staring at the falling leaves
Swirling in the gentle breeze…
AUTUMN has blown into town.

Two weeks later, cold winds sound
Leaves against the windows pound
Sending Onyx and Kramer to the top of the sill
While Tucker remains quite sullen and still.
She can no longer hop to the very top
And as soon as she tries, she's forced to stop.
Her eyes seem sad; her face looks pale
Her once strong body is now so frail.
She sends the household into a flurry
Ms. E becomes so full of worry.
Tucker slowly moves away
From food, from light, from fun and play.

Silence falls on Station Lane
Amidst the gentle sound of rain
The house is quiet—not a peep.
Night has brought the gift of sleep.
Ms. E awakens close to dawn
She brushes her teeth and stifles a yawn
And readies to brew her morning cup
No one is stirring; no one is up.

She passes by an open door
And sees Poor Tucker on the floor.
She cradles the cat and kisses her head
But knows in her heart that TUCKER IS DEAD.

She wraps her in a flannel sheet
And lays her down upon a seat
Calling Kramer and Onyx with a deep, deep sigh
She brings them near to say "Good-bye"
Then buries the cat behind the shed
And takes herself back up to bed
Kramer and Onyx remain in their places
With sadness and sorrow marked on their faces
Grateful they are to have one another
For each to the other can now be a BROTHER.

WINTER

Autumn fades; the leaves are down
And Onyx wears a little frown
He mourns his sister all day long
Life without her seems so wrong
Kramer the King accepts the loss
And continues to act like he's the boss
The air outside gets very still
And Kramer jumps on the windowsill
Snowflakes start falling from the sky
So Kramer cries "Oh my, Oh my!"
"Onyx, come here and sit with me
Open your eyes and you will see…
WINTER has come to town."
Grieving Tucker in her heart
Ms. E still tries to play her part
Making the home a cozy space
Burning twigs in the fireplace
Stirring soup and making tea
She tries to soothe her family.

The house is comfy, safe and warm
Awaiting the impending storm.
The sky gets dark; the wind blows near
Onyx and Kramer cuddle in fear.
Ms. E delights in watching the two
Forming a friendship that is very new
Kramer so young; Onyx so old
Never expecting what is now to be told…

Two months pass; it's late at night
Ms. feels things are not quite right.
She searches for Onyx in every space
Trying to find his hiding place.
He's not in the hallway; he's not on the stairs
He's not on the sofa; he's not on the chairs
He's not in the closet; he's not near the phone
BUT he's in the corner all all alone.

The next day Onyx refuses to play
He simply wants to sleep all day
Not drinking water, not eating food
Putting Ms. E in worried mood.
She finally decides to call the vet
To diagnose her beloved pet.
"Hurry up and bring him here!"
The vet replies, sensing her fear.
She bundles Onyx in a pillowcase
Jumps in her car and begins to race.

Ms. E arrives with Onyx in hand
Awaiting the appointment that had been planned.
She's strangely filled with a sense of gloom
As Dr. S takes Onyx to the examining room.
Nervously waiting for the return of the vet
Ms. E continues to worry and fret.
The vet emerges and calls Ms. E
Sits her down, and explains gently:
"Onyx is getting old, as you are aware
The best solution is LONG-TERM CARE.

The treatment he'll get will be just right
And visiting hours are day or night."
The news of the doctor takes Ms. E by surprise
She hugs poor Onyx with tears in her eyes.
She says "Goodbye" and returns to her car
The distance home suddenly feels very far.
She pulls into her driveway and there at the door
Kramer awaits her, expecting more.
"Where is Onyx?", he seems to say
So Ms. E calms him down in her peaceful way.
Snow is still falling; the wind chills the bone
Kramer sits on the windowsill now ALL ALONE.

SPRING

The house feels empty; there's little noise
Kramer loses interest in even his toys
Ms. E believes he needs a friend
To bring his sadness to an end.
She gets in her car helter-skelter
And drives herself to the Animal Shelter.
There she sets eyes on a green-eyed cat
Slightly plump but not very fat.
The cat beams a message to Ms. E
"Take me home – PLEASE, TAKE ME!"

Ms. E and her foundling get on the road
And just before reaching her humble abode
Ms. E spies a crocus pushing its head
Through the grass of the neighbor's flowerbed.
SPRING has bloomed in town!

Ms. E brings the new pet into her home
Not knowing the layout, the cat starts to roam
First to the kitchen, then down the stairs
Next up a ladder, then under the chairs.
Ms. E wants to stop this frightening game.
But what shall she call her? – the cat has no name!
Her striped furry tail, her elegant coat
Her bib of white fur reaching up to her throat
Her paws so refined as if made of crystal
Ms. E cannot help but call her "Miss Bristol".

The bathroom becomes her hideaway place
As Miss Bristol adjusts to her very new space.
But Kramer, remember, loves to say "Mine!"
So the new arrangement is not very fine!
He marches forward with jealous rage
"I'll show Ms. E what I'll do to this cage!"
He knows the bathroom gets heavily locked
But Kramer simply won't stand to be blocked.
He hurls his body against the door
And all of his paws come right off the floor!
He screeches, he howls, he simpers, he wails
But try as he might, King Kramer still fails

Ms. E grabs Kramer with all of her might
But he scratches, and claws, and gives her a fight.
Holding him tightly she opens the door
Afraid to release him back down to the floor
Once inside, what does she see?
A frightened Miss B MAKING PEE-PEE!

Faster than lightning shoots from the sky
Kramer pries loose and readies to fly
Right to the litter box, next to the toys
Invading the territory with lots of noise.
Ms. E stands by totally frazzled
Never realizing she's soon to be dazzled.
Miss Bristol comes forward primed for a fight
And whacks King Kramer with all of her might.
They go at each other: SLAP! KICK! SLAP!
Then fall down exhausted – time for a nap.
Miss Bristol is proud that she's brought Kramer down
It's time for the King to SHARE HIS CROWN.

SUMMER

The flowers outside continue to bloom
Ms. E cuts a bunch to put in her room.
Fearing the cats might eat them for lunch
She prepares to gather a second bunch.
But lo and behold—my, oh, my
Miss Bristol and Kramer NOW SEE EYE TO EYE!
Perched on the countertop, peaceful and quiet
Not making a fuss; not causing a riot.
Suddenly acting like sister and brother
And paying attention to one another.
The scent of the flowers, the heat of the day
The sun through the windows, the children at play
SUMMER has moved into town.

Ms. E is delighted the fights are no more
The cats snuggle up on the living room floor.
Licking each other – so tender, so sweet
Sharing their bowls when it's time to eat.
Kramer has finally come in to his own

No longer attached to his crown or his throne.
Miss Bristol, as well, has become more mature
Far more confident, more self-assured.

In her rocking chair, sipping tea
Ms. E remembers what used to be.
She smiles at memories of earlier days
When Kramer's grandiosity was all ablaze.
Thinking with fondness of sister and brother
Onyx and Tucker who cared for each other
And brought such sweetness into her home
And helped her to feel not quite so alone.
Now time has come for Ms. E to pursue
Something exciting, something new.
She buys a piano from the music store
And begins to take lessons from Monsieur Latour.
Mozart's her favorite; Chopin's second best
She's inspired to practice with little rest.
Every evening at 1 Station Lane
Kramer and Bristol are on the window pane
Waiting eagerly for Ms. E to start
To play the music with all of her heart.

The story has now come to its close
With all the characters in sweet repose.
The house on Station Lane holds three
Two LOVING cats and kind Ms. E.